HIS␣␣␣␣Y

This I-SPY book belongs to:_____

Introduction

History is not just about dates and facts in books. It is all around us. We can see it when we go walking or for a ride in a car; we can see it in towns and in the country. Even trees can be witness to the passing of historical events. Take I-Spy History with you the next time you go out and see just how many things there are that tell us about history: anything from caves where people lived at a time when animals such as bears still lived wild in Britain, to the old trams that once clanged through city streets. If you are not sure about where to find some of the things, especially the prehistoric sites, local walking maps will be a great help. Some items are more difficult to spy than others so, if you are going on holiday, why not find out what there is to go and see. But lots of things aren't listed in any guide books, so you will need to keep your eyes open and find them for yourself. And try to imagine what life was like in the places you visit.

With I-Spy History, you'll soon find that history can be fun.

How to use your I-SPY book

I-Spy History has been arranged in chronological order from the different ages of prehistory at the beginning through to modern times at the end. Each era is indicated by the coloured bands at the top of the pages and the approximate date of each era is shown at the start.

Some things which you are asked to I-Spy have been used throughout much of prehistory and history and are included in that section of the book of which they are most typical. You need 1000 points to send off for your I-Spy certificate (see page 64) but that is not

too difficult because there are masses of points in every book. As you make each I-Spy, write your score in the box and, where there is a question, double your score if you can answer it. Check your answer against the correct one on page 63.

I-SPY TITLES AVAILABLE:

CAVE DWELLING

Primitive human-like animals began living in caves about 40,000 years ago during the Ice Age, before the period which we now call the Stone Age. They went out to hunt for animals such as reindeer and mammoths.

In the Ice Age, men used to hunt dinosaurs – True or False?

I-SPY points: 15
Double with answer

Date: _____

STONE AXE

The Stone Age is so called because people living at that time made tools from stone. Stones, such as flint, could be shaped and polished to make axes that could cut down even big trees.

I-SPY points: 15

Date: _____

3

STONE AGE HOUSE

This house was built more than 4,000 years ago. It has a hearth in the centre, stone beds that were filled with bracken and straw and even a stone 'dresser'.

I-SPY points: 25

Date: _____

ANCIENT TRACKWAY

The 'main roads' of prehistoric times often ran along the tops of hills to keep away from the swamps and woods of the valleys. Some, such as the Ridgeway, are still used as footpaths and long-distance trails. Look on your local walking maps to find these ancient tracks.

I-SPY points: 15

Date: _____

CHAMBERED TOMB

In the Stone Age, people began burying their dead in stone chambers, like rooms with stone walls and roof, sometimes covered with earth. The earth has now eroded leaving just the stones. Local walking maps mark some of the tombs.

I-SPY points: 20

Date: _____

LONG BARROW

Another kind of Stone Age burial site was a great mound of earth, sometimes with a stone entrance. This was a long barrow and many people were buried together, with their treasures. Not all long barrows are marked on all local walking maps but these maps should certainly help you find some of them.

I-SPY points: 20

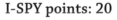

Date: _____

STONE CIRCLES

The earliest stone monuments date back to the Stone Age. No one knows for certain why they are there: most people think they mark religious sites and some people believe they mark magic places where strange, supernatural forces are at work. Sometimes there are many stones together, set out in a ring, such as Hurlers Stone Circle (left) or Stonehenge (below).

I-SPY points: 15 for each

Date: _____

STANDING STONES

Great stones were set up on end after the end of the Stone Age. These are from the Bronze Age.

I-SPY points: 15

Date: _____

ROUND BARROW

In the Bronze Age, which began over 3,000 years ago, the dead were buried under round, earthen humps. Often, you can see many round barrows together, just as you see lots of graves in a modern cemetery. Like the earlier long barrows, some of these are marked on local walking maps.

I-SPY points: 15

Date: _____

I-SPY points: 15

Date: _____

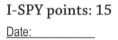

HILL FORT

In the years before the Romans came to Britain, people learned how to make iron tools and their time became known as the Iron Age. To protect themselves from attack, they built hilltop forts, surrounded by banks and ditches. Some hill forts are obvious but there are others which are less easy to spot unless you look for their locations on local walking maps.

IRON AGE HUT

Iron Age people lived in simple round huts with high thatched roofs. Now only the low stone walls are left to mark where the huts once stood. These are usually marked on maps.

I-SPY points: 15

Date: _____

BROCH

In Scotland, Iron Age people called Picts built great round fortresses with double walls that had rooms between them. The biggest broch still stands over 13 metres (43ft) high.

I-SPY points: 20

Date: _____

HILL FIGURES

Hill figures were made by cutting through the grass on chalk hills to show the chalk rock beneath. White horses are the most popular but there are also strange figures of men.

I-SPY points: 20

Date: _____

9

The Roman Occupation AD 43-410

ROMAN VILLA

These grand houses often had colourful, patterned floors made of small pieces of stone, known as mosaic. The picture shows the remains of the underground heating system called a hypercaust.

I-SPY points: 20

Date: _____

ROMAN ROAD

Roman roads are famous for being straight. Sometimes, all we see now are banks going across fields. Often modern roads follow the routes of Roman Roads. In many cases, the route of a Roman road is marked on a local walking map. The A5 from London to Hollyhead is based on the old roman road called Watling Street.

I-SPY points: 15

Date: _____

ROMAN DEFENSIVE WALL

Hadrian's Wall is the best known of the walls built to defend the parts of Britain conquered by the Romans. It is not the only one.

What is the name of the Roman Wall across Scotland?

I-SPY points: 20

Double with answer

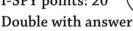

Date: _____

ROMAN AMPHITHEATRE

This was an open-air theatre used for parades, plays, and gladiator battles. Spectators sat on the banks.

I-SPY points: 20

Date: _____

The Roman Occupation

ROMAN FORT

The Romans were invaders and they had to guard important places all over the country. Soldiers lived in forts, sometimes built in very wild places. The remains of this fort can be seen at Housesteads on Hadrian's Wall.

I-SPY points: 20

Date: _____

ROMAN TEMPLE

The Romans built temples in which to worship many different gods. This temple has been rebuilt and it shows how colourful it once was.

I-SPY points: 20

Date: _____

12

SAXON VILLAGE

The Anglo-Saxons first came to Britain over 1,500 years ago. They lived in simple villages with wooden houses. In this village at West Stow, the houses have been reconstructed using traditional Saxon techniques where possible.

I-SPY points: 20

Date: _____

SAXON DEFENCES

To defend themselves and to mark boundaries, the Saxons dug deep ditches or dykes.

I-SPY points: 20

Date: _____

WHAT'S IN A NAME?

During the Dark Ages, especially in the ninth century, Vikings, mainly from what is now Denmark, invaded the British Isles, firstly to make off with whatever they could steal, but then as settlers.

The areas of England that were settled were largely around Yorkshire, East Anglia and in parts of Nottinghamshire, Derbyshire, Leicestershire and Lincolnshire.

The areas that the Danes colonized can be detected today in some of the place names. For example, places that end in '-toft' such as Lowestoft in Suffolk are likely to have been Viking settlements because in Old Danish toft means 'homestead'.

Similarly some place names ending in '-thorpe', such as Scunthorpe in Lincolnshire suggest that the Danes once had a farm or settlement on the site.

Similarly you can work out from their names places which were once Roman towns or villages. For example places where the names end in '-castle' or '-chester' such as Winchester or Lancaster are likely to have been occupied by the Romans because this ending comes from the Latin castra meaning military encampment.

If you want to find out more about the origins of place names, you should be able to find books in your local library, or on the internet.

King Alfred the Great ruled from 871-899 and defended Anglo-Saxon England from the Viking invaders.

LANCASTER CASTLE

I-SPY points: 20

Date: _____

WINCHESTER CATHEDRAL

I-SPY points: 20

Date: _____

BATTLEFIELD

Battlefields are marked on maps by crossed swords. Sometimes, there are exciting re-creations of the battles themselves.

In which famous battle did William the Conqueror defeat the English King Harold in 1066?

I-SPY points: 15
Double with answer

Date: _____

NORMAN CASTLE

Like the Romans and the Anglo-Saxons, the Normans were invaders. They built castles to defend themselves. Because castles were safe places, towns often grew up around them.

I-SPY points: 10

Date: _____

Here are some things to I-Spy in castles:

BATTLEMENTS

Battlements at the tops of walls and towers were built to protect the soldiers during attacks.

I-SPY points: 5

Date: _____

DRAWBRIDGE

A drawbridge across the moat. The bridge could be pulled up if the castle was attacked.

I-SPY points: 5

Date: _____

PORTCULLIS

The portcullis is a strong grille that could be lowered to block a gateway.

I-SPY points: 5

Date: _____

DUNGEON

The dungeon was usually a dark room, beneath the castle, where prisoners were kept.

I-SPY points: 5

Date: _____

CITY WALLS

Old cities were surrounded by high walls, sometimes with walkways, to keep them safe from attack. Gateways allowed people in and out and were heavily defended.

I-SPY points: 15

Date: _____

NORMAN CHURCH

The Normans built many churches. A lot of churches have been altered since, but may still have some parts built by the Normans, such as this round tower. Many churches have little guide books telling you how old all the different bits are, and these help you find the old parts of the church.

I-SPY points: 15

Date: _____

Here are some other things to look for in a church:

CRYPT

Some churches have dark chambers beneath called crypts. Sometimes people were buried in the crypt.

I-SPY points: 5

Date: _____

MONUMENTS AND BRASSES

Some churches have monuments showing for example knights, who went to fight in the Crusades. They can be stone, like this one, or pictures on brass plates. You can make copies of the plates. The copies are called 'brass rubbings'.

Monument
I-SPY points: 5

Date: _____

Brass Plates
I-SPY points: 5

Date: _____

ABBEYS

The abbeys were not just very big churches, they were also places where monks lived, studied and worshipped. Later King Henry VIII ordered them to be destroyed, so many are now left in ruins.

Complete Abbey
I-SPY points: 20

Date: _____

Ruined Abbey
I-SPY points: 15

Date: _____

GARGOYLES

Stand outside the church and look up toward the roof. You might spy strange carved heads or peculiar animals. These are called gargoyles. Gargoyles are always used as drainpipes. The other decorative features are called grotesques.

I-SPY points: 5

Date: _____

CHAINED LIBRARY

Before the printing press was invented, all books were copied by hand. They were very valuable and were chained together in special libraries to keep them safe.

I-SPY points: 20

Date: _____

PALACE

These very grand houses were built as homes for bishops, archbishops, kings and queens.

I-SPY points: 15

Date: _____

TOWER OF LONDON

The central White Tower was founded by William the Conqueror (the last successful invader of Britain) in 1076 on the site of a Roman fort that had been built more than a thousand years earlier.

I-SPY points: 15

Date: _____

WINDSOR CASTLE

Originally built by William the Conqueror between 1070 and 1086 AD, Windsor Castle is the largest inhabited castle in the world.

I-SPY points: 15

Date:

SUIT OF ARMOUR

The full suit of armour was worn by knights who fought on horseback to protect them in battle.

I-SPY points: 20

Date:

SWORD

Swords have been used in battles for thousands of years. This is a heavy two-handed sword which stood almost as high as the man who used it.

I-SPY points: 5

Date:

BATTLE AXE

Battle axes and battle hammers were also used by knights on horseback.

I-SPY points: 5

Date:

SHIELD

Shields, used for protection, were often decorated in many different ways.

I-SPY points: 5

Date:

THATCHED ROOF

Roofs made of straw, reeds or other plants, such as heather, have been in use for thousands of years.

I-SPY points: 10

Date:

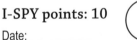

SUN DIAL

The sun dial was used for telling the time long before clocks were invented. The time is shown by the shadow of the upstanding arm cast by the sun on to the graduated dial.

What is the name of the upstanding arm on a sundial?

I-SPY points: 15

Double with answer

Date: _____

TITHE BARN

Tithe means 'tenth'. Once farmers had to give a tenth of everything they grew to the Church and the grain was kept in tithe barns. They are much bigger than ordinary farm barns.

I-SPY points: 15

Date: _____

WORKING HORSES

Once, horses did all the work on a farm that is now done mainly by tractors and other machines. Some of today's farmers are returning to the use of working horses.

I-SPY points: 15

Date:

BLACKSMITH

Horses wear metal horseshoes to protect their hooves. The blacksmith shapes the hot metal on the anvil, then nails the horse shoe to the hoof. This does not hurt the horse. Because we still use horses today you can find working blacksmiths.

I-SPY points: 15

Date:

TIMBER-FRAMED HOUSE

The house was first built as a wooden frame then all the spaces in the walls were filled in with brick or other materials. As the wood ages in bends in different ways giving these houses a strange appearance.

I-SPY points: 10

Date: _____

DOVECOTE

People kept doves and pigeons in special buildings called dovecotes. The birds and their eggs were used for food. Today, we usually keep hens and chickens instead.

I-SPY points: 15

Date: _____

WATERMILL

There used to be thousands of working watermills in Britain. The waterwheels turned the grindstones that ground the corn into flour.

I-SPY points: 15

Date: _____

WATERWHEEL

In time, waterwheels were used to power all kinds of machinery, in many different industries. The type of wheel shown here is called an overshot wheel, because the water falls over the top of it. This wheel is actually from the nineteenth century.

I-SPY points: 15

Date: _____

WINDMILL

Most windmills were used for grinding corn. This is a post mill. The whole mill balances on a post and can be swung around to face the wind. Sometimes the sails are fixed to a cap at the top of the mill. Then the mill is known as a tower mill if the tower is brick or stone, or a smock mill if it is wood. Windmills were still being built as recently as 100 years ago.

I-SPY points: 15

Date: _____

TUDOR SHIP

The Mary Rose was part of Henry VIII's navy and was raised from under the sea. The picture shows the ship as it once looked.

You can also see copies of other old ships, as well as models, in museums. As these type of ships were made of wood, very few survive.

I-SPY points: 20

Date: _____

SPINNING WHEEL

The wheel was used to make the fleeces of sheep into wool for knitting or for weaving into cloth. The spinning was mainly done by women working at home.

I-SPY points: 15

Date: _____

LOOM

The loom is used to turn yarn, such as wool, into cloth. Once the work was done on hand looms like this one; now it is done mostly in factories on big machines.

What do we call people who make cloth on a loom?

I-SPY points: 15
Double with answer

Date: _____

PACKHORSE BRIDGE

These bridges generally have high arches and are very narrow. They were not wide enough for carts, but were used by horses that carried goods on their backs.

I-SPY points: 15

Date: _____

COBBLED STREET

Before tarmac was invented, stones called 'cobbles' or 'setts' were used for road making. Cobbled streets are very uneven and make wheels rattle as they go over them.

I-SPY points: 15

Date: _____

STOCKS

This was an old form of punishment. People's feet were locked in the stocks, and they were pelted with rotten fruit and bad eggs.

I-SPY points: 15

Date: _____

CANNON

Cannon were used on ships of all kinds and by armies on land. They were mounted on wheels, and fired solid cannon balls, not explosive shells. They can often be found around the coast as decorative features now.

I-SPY points: 15

Date: _____

FIGUREHEAD

A figurehead was a bust or statue that was put on the bows of the ship. It made the ship look beautiful and was also meant to bring good luck.

I-SPY points: 15

Date: _____

FOUR POSTER BED

Old houses were often very draughty. With a four poster bed, you could pull curtains all around the bed to keep you warm at night and to cut out the light.

I-SPY points: 15

Date: _____

MILESTONE

The new roads of the eighteenth century had milestones, marked with numbers of miles, to show distances of the next town.

I-SPY points: 15

Date: _____

TOLL ROADS AND HOUSES

In the eighteenth century, hundreds of miles of new roads with good surfaces were built. Many were private roads and travellers had to pay to use them. The traveller paid his or her money at a toll house which stood at a junction or at a bridge and jutted out into the road so that money was easy to collect from carts and carriages.

I-SPY points: 15

Date: _____

HOT AIR BALLOON

The first men flew in balloons over 200 years ago and in 1785 the first crossing of the English channel was made by balloon.

I-SPY points: 15

Date: _____

SIGNPOST

These old-fashioned signposts were just the right height for someone mounted on a horse to read easily.

I-SPY points: 15

Date: _____

STAGE COACH

Coaches took passengers on long journeys, changing horses along the way. Each set of horses worked for one stage of the journey. This is a mail coach which also carried letters and parcels.

I-SPY points: 20

Date: _____

SEDAN CHAIR

The sedan chair was used in towns. Passengers got in and two men lifted the chair on poles and carried it through the streets. This meant rich people didn't have to walk on the often filthy streets.

I-SPY points: 20

Date: _____

CANAL

In the days before railways, canals were the most efficient way of moving heavy goods. One horse pulling a boat could move as much as twenty-five horses pulling carts along the road. Now most canals are used for recreation.

I-SPY points: 10

Date: _____

WORKING CANAL BOAT

Boats such as this one are called narrow boats. The cargo was loaded in the front and the family lived in the tiny cabins at the back.

I-SPY points: 10

Date: _____

LOCK

A lock is necessary when there is an incline on the canal. When a boat goes into a lock, the gates are closed behind it and the boat goes up or down as the water is let in or out. The first canal lock in Britain was built more than 400 years ago.

I-SPY points: 10

Date: _____

IRON BRIDGE

The first iron bridge in Britain was built in 1781 at the place now called Ironbridge. This was built by Thomas Telford.

Which river does it cross?

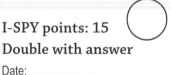

I-SPY points: 15
Double with answer

Date: _____

TEXTILE MILL

The first cotton and woollen mills were built over 200 years ago. Early mills like this one were worked by a water wheel. Many young children worked in the mill.

I-SPY points: 15

Date: _____

WATER PUMP

We now get water by turning a tap but it used to come from a well or was pumped up by hand. Often there was just one pump for the whole village. Villages grew according the the ready supply of water, the prime necessity of life.

I-SPY points: 15

Date: _____

LOCK UP

Many villages had special buildings, like very small prisons where people who misbehaved were locked up for the night or longer.

I-SPY points: 20

Date: _____

SAILING SHIP

Because Britain is an island, merchants had to use ships for trade. Sailing ships were sent out to all parts of the world. Britain has a rich maritime history.

I-SPY points: 20

Date: _____

COMMUNICATIONS

Samuel Morse invented Morse code in 1838. It revolutionised communication and allowed for messages to be passed over great distances. The first telegraph message followed in 1858.

What were the two places joined by the first transatlantic message?

I-SPY points: 25
Double with answer

Date: _____

OIL LAMP

Once the only way to light a house at nights was to use candles or an oil lamp. A piece of cloth, called a wick, dips into the oil. It soaks up the oil so that the top of the wick can be set alight to burn slowly. Gas lamps have to be lit by hand. This was a danger and caused many fires if the lamp was knocked over.

I-SPY points: 15

Date: _____

GAS WORKS

Today we use natural gas but 200 years ago gas was made by burning coal at a special gas works. The buildings are now often ruins but the big gas holders can still be seen. These are known as gasometers – the one shown here is almost empty.

I-SPY points: 15

Date: _____

GAS LIGHT

At first gas was used for lighting streets and houses. Later it was used for heating and cooking. Gas lamps have to be lit by hand.

Internal I-SPY points: 20

Date: _____

External I-SPY points: 20

Date: _____

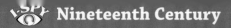
COAL HOLE COVER

Many old houses had coal cellars. The metal cover was lifted and the coal tipped down the hole, allowing the coal to be removed from the inside of the house. Some covers are square, some round and they often have patterns on them.

I-SPY points: 15

Date: _____

STEAM ENGINE

Steam engines were once used to work the machinery of factories and mills. Some have been specially preserved and can be as much as 200 years old.

I-SPY points: 20

Date: _____

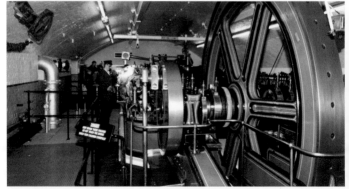

FACTORY CHIMNEY

Coal was burned in big boilers to heat the water to make steam for engines. The smoke from the furnace escaped up the tall chimney, but some of the residue fell to the earth as soot.

I-SPY points: 15

Date: _____

COAL MINE

There are still some coal mines at work but a lot have closed. Some are now open to visitors who are taken underground.

I-SPY points: 15

Date: _____

SLATE MINES

Not all mines are coal mines. This mine produced slate which was used for roofing.

I-SPY points: 15

Date: _____

TIN MINES

During the 19th century, Cornwall had over 2,000 tin mines and exported tin all around the world. There are many types of mines from gold to lead.

I-SPY points: 15

Date: _____

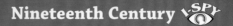

IRON WORKS

There are two kinds of iron works: foundries, where hot metal is poured into moulds and forges, where metal is shaped by hitting it with big hammers. The hammers in forges would have been powered by a water mill.

I-SPY points: 15

Date: _____

POTTERY KILN

Pots are made from clay and baked in a kiln. This type of kiln is known as a bottle kiln because of its shape.

I-SPY points: 20

Date: _____

49

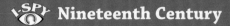

MARTELLO TOWER

These costal defence towers were built when it was thought that France, led by Napoleon, was going to invade England.

I-SPY points: 20

Date: _____

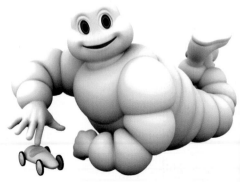

STEAM LOCOMOTIVE

The first steam locomotive ran on a railway in 1802. Now they can be seen at work on preserved railways on special trips.

I-SPY points: 15

Date: _____

QUEEN VICTORIA

Born in 1819, Victoria became Queen at 18 years old and ruled over a period of huge change. She reigned longer than any other British Monarch and longer than any female in history.

How long did Queen Victoria reign?

I-SPY points: 15

Double with answer

Date: _____

DISUSED RAILWAYS

The invention of the railway allowed people and goods to be easily transported all over the country. Many railways are no longer used, the tracks have been dismantled and some are now used for footpaths. Along the way you can often see signals, signs and even stations.

I-SPY points: 15

Date: _____

TRACTION ENGINE

Steam engines were used on the road in the nineteenth century to pull heavy loads. Today you can see them at special steam fairs.

I-SPY points: 15

Date: _____

PADDLE STEAMER

The first ships to use steam power were paddle streamers. They became very popular for trips around the coast and on some lakes.

I-SPY points: 15

Date: _____

CARGO STEAMER

After paddles, steamers had propellers to drive them through the water. The first big steamer to have a propeller was the SS Great Britain, built by I. K. Brunell.

I-SPY points: 15

Date: _____

FLORENCE NIGHTINGALE

Born in 1820 Florence trained as a nurse. In 1854 she went to care for solders in the Crimea war with a band of nurses and was afterwards known as 'The Lady with the Lamp'.

I-SPY points: 15

Date: _____

VICTORIAN POST BOX

The first postage stamp was used in Britain in 1840. For the first time people could buy a stamp, stick it on a letter and post it in one of the new post boxes. The oldest have the initials VR for Victoria Regina or Queen Victoria.

I-SPY points: 15

Date: _____

I. K. BRUNELL

Born in 1806, Isambard Kingdom Brunell was the greatest engineer of the Victorian era. His inventions included tunnels, bridges and ships.

I-SPY points: 20 for any Brunell structure

Date: _____

OMNIBUS

The first horse dawn omnibus was seen in the streets of London more than 150 years ago. The modern omnibus has a motor and its name has been shortened to bus.

I-SPY points: 15

Date: _____

TRAM

Street trams look like buses but they run on rails. They were originally pulled by horses but later they were powered by electricity. The first electric trams in Britain ran about 100 years ago. Blackpool is famous for trams running along the seafront.

I-SPY points: 15

Date: _____

MENAI SUSPENSION BRIDGE

One of the first modern suspension bridges, it was designed by Thomas Telford. Construction began in 1820 and the bridge opened in 1826, becoming on the main trade route between Britain and Ireland.

I-SPY points: 25, any other suspension bridge for 10 points

Date: _____

PENNY FARTHING

This strange looking bicycle got its name from two coins because one wheel was like an old penny and the other was tiny like a farthing.

I-SPY points: 20

Date: _____

LONDON UNDERGROUND

London's underground railway, or the Tube, was the world's first underground railway system. The service between Paddington Station and Farringdon Street opened in 1863.

I-SPY points: 10

Date: _____

AEROPLANES

Before the invention of the jet engine all aeroplanes had propellers. The first aeroplane with an engine flew in 1902, the Wright brothers claimed the first manned flight in 1903. This plane has two sets of wings one above the other.

What is this type of aeroplane called?

I-SPY points: 15
Double with answer
Date:

TANK

Tanks were first used at the British battle of the Somme in 1916. Tanks have caterpillar tracks so that they can go over rough ground. Modern tanks have guns fixed to a turret which can turn in any direction.

I-SPY points: 15
Date:

PILL BOX

This is a small fort for soldiers. It was built as a defence against invaders. It got its name because it looks like an old-fashioned box in which pills were sold.

I-SPY points: 15

Date: _____

WORLD WAR I AEROPLANE

This was the first war in which aeroplanes took part. In Britain the Royal Flying Corps was formed and it later became the Royal Air Force.

I-SPY points: 15

Date: _____

BATTLESHIPS

Modern Battleships have guns mounted on turrets. This World War II battleship could hit a target over 23km (14 miles) away.

I-SPY points: 15

Date: _____

WORLD WAR II AEROPLANE

One of the most important battles of World War II was the Battle of Britain, fought in the air. Many of the old aeroplanes still fly on Battle of Britain Day and other commemorative events.

I-SPY points: 15

Date: _____

HELICOPTER

Many attempts were made to build a fully working helicopter during the early 20th century, but it was not until 1942 that the first models reached full scale production. Today helicopters are used for all kinds of work including the rescue services.

I-SPY points: 15

Date: _____

HOVERCRAFT

The first 'real' hovercraft was designed by Sir Christopher Cockerell and launched in 1959. 'Floating' on a cushion of air, it skimmed across the top of the water and is much faster than a ship or boat.

I-SPY points: 20

Date: _____

Compared to various kinds of trees, the human life span is quite short and many generations of people may live and die during the life of say an Oak tree or especially a Yew.

There are Yew trees growing in Britain today that are at least 1000 years old. This means that they were alive and well when William the Conqueror came to Britain in 1066.

You will often find old Yew trees in churchyards. No one knows for sure why this should be so but Yew wood was much in demand by craftsmen of medieval times for making the famous English longbow and some have suggested that Yew trees once had a religious significance. Remember, however, that all parts of the Yew tree, except for the red flesh of the berries are very poisonous so it made sense to plant Yews in the churchyard where they were less likely to be eaten by cattle or young children.

The clipped Yew trees in this picture grow in the churchyard at Painswick near Stroud in Gloucestershire. Legend has it that there are 99 trees and that the devil always prevents a hundredth tree from growing. These Yews were planted in 1792, the same year that the French Revolution overthrew the monarchy and France became a republic.

Don't forget that almost any big tree may well be several hundred years old. It is said by country people that an Oak takes ...300 years agrowin', 300 years alivin', and 300 years a-dyin'! So look around you, in your garden, in the local parks or woods and you may well find trees that have witnessed as much as 1000 years of British history from the coming of the Normans, to the English Civil War, from before the London Blitz, right up to the present day.

Index

First published by Michelin Maps and Guides 2010
© Michelin, Proprietaires-Editeurs 2010.
Michelin and the Michelin Man are registered
Trademarks of Michelin.
Created and produced by Horizons Publishing Limited.
All rights reserved. No part of this publication may be
reproduced, copied or transmitted in any form without
the prior consent of the publisher. Print services by
FingerPrint International Book production - fingerprint@
pandora.beThe publisher gratefully acknowledges the
contribution of the I-Spy team: Camilla Lovell, Sheila
Watts and Ruth Neilson in the production of this title.
The publisher gratefully acknowledges the contribution
and assistance of the sites and attractions in the
book, plus F. Scott Crawford, Tom Blackwell, Britain on
View, St. Edmundsbury Borough Council, Leicestershire
Promotions Ltd, Alisa Beth Mix, Jeffrey L Thomas,
Bill Tyne, The Mary Rose Trust, Ruth Nolan, Glen
Clapstow, Angus Kirk, Ruth Nolan, Robert H Wyatt,
National Maritime Museum, Graham Ransden, unitaw,
Janice Lane, Tom Blackwell, Geoff Hunt, Black Country
Living Museum, Imperial War Museum, London
Transport Museum, National Museum of Wales, The
Tank Museum, R.N.L.I. and Ros Wood who provided
the photographs in this book. Other images in the public
domain and used under a creative commons license.

Answers: P3 Cave Dwelling, False, **P11** Roman Defensive Wall, The Antonine Wall, **P16** Battlefield, The Battle of Hastings, **P27** Sun Dial, Gnomon, **P33** Loom, Weavers, **P41** Ironbridge, River Severn, **P43** Communications, Newfoundland and Ireland, **P51** Queen Victoria, Reigned for 63 years, **P58** Aeroplanes, Bi-plane

HOW TO GET YOUR I-SPY CERTIFICATE AND BADGE

Every time you score 1000 points or more in an I-Spy book, you can apply for a certificate

HERE'S WHAT TO DO, STEP BY STEP:

Certificate

- Ask an adult to check your score

- Ask his or her permission to apply for a certificate

- Apply online to www.ispymichelin.com

- Enter your name and address and the completed title

- We will send you back via e mail your certificate for the title

Badge

- Each I-Spy title has a cut out (page corner) token at the back of the book

- Collect five tokens from different I-Spy titles

- Put Second Class Stamps on two strong envelopes

- Write your own address on one envelope and put a £1 coin inside it (for protection). Fold, but do not seal the envelope, and place it inside the second envelope

- Write the following address on the second envelope, seal it carefully and post to:

I-Spy Books
Michelin Maps and Guides
Hannay House
39 Clarendon Road
Watford
WD17 1JA